I0455855

Editor-in-Chief and Founder:
  Lyndon H. LaRouche, Jr.
Editorial Board: *Lyndon H. LaRouche, Jr. , Helga
  Zepp-LaRouche, Robert Ingraham, Tony
  Papert, Gerald Rose, Dennis Small, Jeffrey
  Steinberg, William Wertz*
Co-Editors: *Robert Ingraham, Tony Papert*
Managing Editor: *Nancy Spannaus*
Technology: *Marsha Freeman*
Books: *Katherine Notley*
Ebooks: *Richard Burden*
Graphics: *Alan Yue*
Photos: *Stuart Lewis*
Circulation Manager: *Stanley Ezrol*

INTELLIGENCE DIRECTORS
Counterintelligence: *Jeffrey Steinberg, Michele
  Steinberg*
Economics: *John Hoefle, Marcia Merry Baker,
  Paul Gallagher*
History: *Anton Chaitkin*
Ibero-America: *Dennis Small*
Russia and Eastern Europe: *Rachel Douglas*
United States: *Debra Freeman*

INTERNATIONAL BUREAUS
Bogotá: *Miriam Redondo*
Berlin: *Rainer Apel*
Copenhagen: *Tom Gillesberg*
Houston: *Harley Schlanger*
Lima: *Sara Madueño*
Melbourne: *Robert Barwick*
Mexico City: *Gerardo Castilleja Chávez*
New Delhi: *Ramtanu Maitra*
Paris: *Christine Bierre*
Stockholm: *Ulf Sandmark*
United Nations, N.Y.C.: *Leni Rubinstein*
Washington, D.C.: *William Jones*
Wiesbaden: *Göran Haglund*

ON THE WEB
e-mail: eirns@larouchepub.com
www.larouchepub.com
www.executiveintelligencereview.com
www.larouchepub.com/eiw
Webmaster: *John Sigerson*
Assistant Webmaster: *George Hollis*
Editor, Arabic-language edition: *Hussein Askary*

EIR (ISSN 0273-6314) *is published weekly
(50 issues), by EIR News Service, Inc.,
P.O. Box 17390, Washington, D.C. 20041-0390.
(703) 777-9451*

European Headquarters: E.I.R. GmbH, Postfach
Bahnstrasse 9a, D-65205, Wiesbaden, Germany
Tel: 49-611-73650
Homepage: http://www.eirna.com
e-mail: eirna@eirna.com
Director: Georg Neudecker

Montreal, Canada: 514-461-1557

Denmark: EIR - Danmark, Sankt Knuds Vej 11,
basement left, DK-1903 Frederiksberg, Denmark.
Tel.: +45 35 43 60 40, Fax: +45 35 43 87 57. e-mail:
eirdk@hotmail.com.

Mexico City: EIR, Sor Juana Inés de la Cruz 242-2
Col. Agricultura C.P. 11360
Delegación M. Hidalgo, México D.F.
Tel. (5525) 5318-2301
eirmexico@gmail.com

Canada Post Publication Sales Agreement
#40683579

Postmaster: Send all address changes to *EIR*, P.O.
Box 17390, Washington, D.C. 20041-0390.

Signed articles in *EIR* represent the views of the
authors, and not necessarily those of the Editorial
Board.

LaRouche's Last-Chance Initiative

EDITORIAL

Drama Infernale … and LaRouche's Deutsche Bank Initiative As the Only Way Out

July 17—The world is facing a *Drama Infernale*, the lead article in the economics section of today's edition of Germany's *Welt am Sonntag* stated in its headline. Not only is the Italian banking system about to blow apart, with 360 billion euros in non-performing loans, but the entire European financial system is bankrupt as well—with derivatives-laden Deutsche Bank at the top of the list—they report nervously.

But the reality is far worse than even that alarmed account suggests. The entire trans-Atlantic financial system has come apart, Lyndon LaRouche noted in a discussion with associates this weekend, and reported at the outset of the July 16 Manhattan Project Dialogue. As LaRouche PAC's Dennis Speed summarized LaRouche's comments:

> The system does not allow for any one point of safety. Don't depend on rational responses from some group. This thing is on the verge of a general global crisis. Therefore, the behavior of people is that they are absolutely panicked; you aren't going to get a rational response at this point. Don't try to depend on anyone, don't try to select any individual. This is an emergency situation, with an emergency problem and we have to address it from that standpoint.

That emergency action centers on LaRouche's call to use a one-time rescue reorganization of Deutsche Bank, based on the principles of the assassinated banker Alfred Herrhausen, to ignite a bankruptcy transformation of the entire trans-Atlantic financial system and unleash actual human productivity.

In further discussion on Sunday, LaRouche stated:

"We have to have an affirmative policy of hyperactive productivity. *You have to create productivity*, real productivity, not somebody holding their money, or their betting money. And the question is: Are we going to create the elements of productivity which are needed in order to get free of what has happened to us by the people who have tried to suppress things and avert things all along? That's where the problem comes. And therefore if you don't assert a policy based on those principles, you are just going to find yourself in the same old mess again."

"We've got to affect all persons," LaRouche continued, "because if they are not in concert in terms of what they are concerned about, then you have anarchy. And that's going back to zero, or less than zero. That's the problem. This is the issue. This is what you have to respond to. If you are not responding to that, you are nothing, you have completely thrown away all kinds of rationality. And that's the only way you can deal with it."

In our international campaign to implement LaRouche's dramatic Deutsche Bank initiative, Helga Zepp-LaRouche noted, we are running into unexpected levels of rage in the population across Europe against Deutsche Bank and *all* bankers, rage which gets in the way of their comprehending LaRouche's call.

"In Germany we had an unprecedented, really unexpected wave of hatred against Deutsche Bank," Zepp-LaRouche noted. "Conservative industrialists, long-term supporters (whom you had never expected to say something like that), they had a completely violent reaction and said: 'Let them go bankrupt! Shut them down! Why should we spend another penny to save these criminal crooks?' And I think that is what people are not fighting through.

"Because the Herrhausen principle is not just saving Deutsche Bank; it's with a gun to the head saying: Either you accept the paradigm shift or you all go under, we all go under with you. But if you want to survive, you have to accept this shift. And if we had an international campaign—which we have a little bit—but if we had a real campaign, the pressure would get greater on the German government, which is the place where the pressure has to end up."

Lyndon LaRouche likewise stressed the importance of the Deutsche Bank reorganization policy: "Emphasize that again, because that's the story. That's exactly what you have to deal with, and that's what you have to fight against."

EIR Contents

www.larouchepub.com Volume 43, Number 30, July 22, 2016

Cover This Week

Lyndon H. LaRouche, Jr.

I. Deutsche Bank Must Be Saved For the Sake of World Peace

WEBCAST WITH ZEPP-LAROUCHE

Bank Rescue Plan Is Last Chance

LaRouche PAC International Webcast (edited), July 15, 2016

Matthew Ogden: Good evening! It's July 15th, 2016. My name is Matthew Ogden, and you're joining us for our weekly webcast on larouchepac.com. I'm joined in the studio tonight by Benjamin Deniston; and we're joined by a very special guest, via live video, Mrs. Helga Zepp-LaRouche. Helga Zepp-LaRouche is the founder of the Schiller Institutes, and also Chairwoman of the German BüSo (Bürgerrechts-bewegung Solidarität, Civil Rights Movement Solidarity) political party.

Helga LaRouche is joining us tonight to discuss the initiative that she and Mr. Lyndon LaRouche have taken this week to act in a very decisive manner to avert World War III and a global economic blow-out. This concerns the situation that Deutsche Bank now finds itself in.

I would like to begin by reading a Statement that Mrs. LaRouche issued a few days ago, on July 12 this week. We will then follow that Statement by a discussion with Mrs. LaRouche herself. In the Statement that Mrs. LaRouche issued, titled "Deutsche Bank Must be Rescued, for the Sake of World Peace," Helga wrote the following:

The imminent threat of the bankruptcy of

video grab/Stuart Lewis

Helga Zepp-LaRouche addressing the July 15, 2016 LaRouche PAC webcast, via video hookup.

Deutsche Bank is certainly not the only potential trigger for a new systemic crisis of the trans-Atlantic banking system, which would be orders of magnitude more deadly than the 2008 crisis, but it does offer a unique lever to prevent a collapse into chaos.

Behind the SOS launched by the chief economist of Deutsche Bank, David Folkerts-Landau, for an EU program of 150 billion euros to recapitalize the banks, lurks the danger openly discussed in international financial media, that the entire European banking system is *de facto* insolvent, and is sitting on a mountain of at least 2 trillion euros of non-performing loans. Deutsche Bank is the international bank which, with a total of 55 trillion euros of outstanding derivative contracts and a leverage factor of 40:1, even outdoes Lehman Brothers at the time of its collapse, and therefore represents the most dangerous Achilles' heel of the system. Half of Deutsche Bank's balance sheet, which has plummeted 48% in the past 12 months and is down to only 8% of its peak value, is made up of Level-3 derivatives, i.e., derivatives amounting to circa 800 billion euros without a market valuation.

It probably came as a surprise to many that

Lyndon LaRouche called today for Deutsche Bank to be saved through a one-time increase in its capital base, because of the systemic implications of its threatened bankruptcy. Neither the German government with its GDP of 4 trillion euros, nor the EU with a GDP of 18 trillion euros, would be able to control the domino effect of a disorderly bankruptcy.

The one-time capital injection, LaRouche explained, is only an emergency measure which needs to be followed by an immediate re-orientation of the bank, back to its tradition which prevailed until 1989 under the leadership of Alfred Herrhausen. To actually oversee such an operation, a management committee must be set up to verify the legitimacy and the implications of the obligations, and finalize its work within a given timeframe. That committee should also draw up a new business plan, based on Herrhausen's banking philosophy and exclusively oriented to the interests of the real economy of Germany.

Alfred Herrhausen was the last actually creative, moral industrial banker of Germany. He defended, among other things, the cancellation of the unpayable debt of developing countries, as well as the long-term credit financing of well-defined development projects. In December 1989, he planned to present in New York a plan for the industrialization of Poland, which was consistent with the criteria

CC/Simsalabimbam

Deutsche Bank headquarters in Frankfurt, Germany.

CC/Karsten11

Kreditanstalt für Wiederaufbau central office in Frankfurt, Germany.

used by the Kreditanstalt für Wiederaufbau (KfW) for the post-1945 reconstruction of Germany, and would have offered a completely different perspective than the so-called "reform policy," or "shock therapy," of Jeffrey Sachs....

Helga completes this Statement by saying:

Herrhausen's assassination has gone unpunished. However, there exists "the dreaded might, that judges what is hid from sight," which is the subject of Friedrich Schiller's poem *Die Kraniche des Ibykus.* The Erinyes have begun their dreadful dance.

It is now incumbent upon all those who, in addition to the family, have suffered from the assassination of Herrhausen, upon the representatives of the Mittelstand, of the German economy and the institutional representatives of the German population, to honor his legacy and to seize the tremendous opportunity which is now offered to save Germany.

With that said, Helga, would you like to follow up at all with any opening statements?

Being 'Against' is Not Enough

Helga Zepp-LaRouche: Well, I think that it is absolutely known to everybody in the international financial community and to all governments and all relevant people in political positions in the trans-Atlantic sector, that what I'm saying there is absolutely true. In other words: the bankers and those responsible for the international financial system all know that this system is absolutely bankrupt, hopelessly bankrupt. It's about to blow up in a much, much bigger way than 2008, for the very simple reason that all indicators which were there before Lehman Brothers and AIG went under, are there, but much more.

The famous tool box which they were using, or pretending to use, in 2008, has been used up: quantitative easing, zero interest rate, negative interest rate, helicopter money. Right now you have the situation—and we have this from extremely reliable contacts in the banking community who agree with us—in which all the central banks are printing money, paper money, like crazy, because they know perfectly well that helicopter money is not just electronic, but if you had a banking run right now, the whole thing would evaporate within a very short period of time, within hours.

This is a situation where if you have an uncontrolled, chaotic collapse, which is right now imminently possible, because you have several triggers,— not only Deutsche Bank. You have the Italian banking sector about to blow. You have the British situation after the Brexit. The entire European banking system is absolutely bankrupt. If you had an uncontrolled collapse, as one banker told us after he read this statement of mine: "If this is not remedied in the short term, we are looking towards a Europe of chaos, disorder, and revolution."

The biggest danger, apart from World War III directly, would be a plunge of the trans-Atlantic sector into chaos. Therefore, my husband—who has a unique record of being right, in terms of forecasting, and being unique, in terms of coming up with proposals for how to remedy the situation—made this very surprising comment: that Deutsche Bank, of all banks, should be singled out, they should be saved, one last time, but not without conditions: They must immediately be put in a sort of receivership. A management commission should be in charge. And then they need a new business plan, which must go back to the philosophy of Alfred Herrhausen, who was the last moral banker in all of Europe, and who had a completely different philosophy.

We had all kinds of reactions about that. It turned out the banks are much more hated than meets the public eye. People said, "Let these banks go bankrupt! Why don't you just close them down? Nationalize them! Bankrupt them!" You had an outpouring of anger coming from people you would not expect—conservative industrialists, politicians who don't normally speak in radical tones at all—but what came out was an explosion of anger.

It is very easy to be angry about the situation. If this thing collapses in an uncontrolled fashion, all the life-savings of people will be ruined. The majority of the people will have to pay, and this will be associated with poverty. Millions of people dying. This is not a joke.

It's not enough to be "against" something; even if banks have behaved completely criminally and immorally. Deutsche Bank is now spending such enormous amounts of money on legal fines for illegal activity from LIBOR swindles, and all kinds of shady operations, that they had to write down their projected profits. It's not a question of "doing a favor" to Deutsche Bank. Not at all! The question is: you must find leverage for how to bring this thing into order, before the whole thing ends up in a collapse, causing an absolute uncontrollable situation.

That is why the reference to Alfred Herrhausen is really extremely important, because he was the head of Deutsche Bank. He was a banker. Deutsche Bank had a different policy, and therefore, when you say, "We have to back to the philosophy of Alfred Herrhausen," at least the older generation knows exactly what that means. Therefore, I think we should really circulate this Statement and force people to put pressure on the situation, for this to be done. You have to "unwind" the outstanding derivatives. You have to deal with the situation that Deutsche Bank has 55 trillion euros in outstanding derivatives. Half of their balance sheet is without market valuation, which means that it's practically worth nothing, because you can't really sell it.

If you have an uncontrolled collapse, then that could be really what brings down the whole thing in a chaotic way. If you go the way Mr. LaRouche has proposed, then you can have an orderly resolution of this bankrupt system, and replace it with one which is in the interest of the people. So, it's not just a technical proposal. Several people, in response to my statement, said, "This is probably the very last chance we have to prevent a catastrophe."

Ogden: Helga, maybe you could also say a little bit more about what the strategic context of this intervention is, especially from the standpoint of the role that Germany plays, not only as the only viable economy in Europe right now, but also the emphasis that Mr. LaRouche has placed on the relationship between Germany and Russia, being the only means by which we can prevent the outbreak of a thermonuclear conflict.

The Real Issue

Zepp-LaRouche: People now have all kinds of proposals, like "Tobin Tax," "tax the speculators"—all these proposals are floating around. What they don't consider, is that when we're talking about banking, we're not talking about money or financial questions; we're taking about the physical pre-condition for a society to exist. Fortunately, the German economy,— despite all of these paradigm shifts for the worse which have occurred in the last 25 years,— the German economy is still an economic powerhouse. You still have a very large concentration of very productive middle-level industry. Middle-level industry is normally where all the patterns are made, the technological innovation occurs. That is really the backbone of the productive economy.

The question is: this German economy, without which all of Europe would not function, absolutely must be protected, and not only be protected,—because right now, it is already many, many small firms that are in danger. There are other factors, like the crazy nuclear energy exit of Mrs. Merkel, which has increased the price of energy tremendously. So the German economy is weakened; but it is still the absolutely crucial factor, because in Germany you have a lot of the industrial potential which is needed not only for all of Europe; but in order to get the whole question of Eurasian cooperation on a sound ground, you need the German economy. The whole question of the German-Russian cooperation, German-Chinese cooperation in the development of the Eurasian Silk Road, is absolutely crucial.

So, the question is the productivity. And what has happened with the paradigm shift of all the successors of Herrhausen—I don't want to name all of them—but all of them went into this high-risk maximization of profit no matter what. Ackermann wanted 25% profit, preferably every month; and they went into these completely crazy derivative operations, so that Deutsche Bank is today *the* leading bank in terms of derivative exposure. With 55 trillion euros in outstanding derivatives, that's with a GDP of the German economy of 4 trillion euros a year; it's over 10 times more, even 12 times more than the GDP of the German economy. So Deutsche Bank long has ceased to be Deutsche Bank; it's now operating from London, from New York. It has become one of the most aggressive investment banks in the world. But if it goes bankrupt, which it could at any moment,— and that's why its chief economist Mr. Folkerts-Landau has put out every day since

David Folkerts-Landau, Global Head of Research at Deutsche Bank, at the European Financial Integration Conference on April 25, 2016.

Sunday, an urgent call saying a recapitalization of the European banks must occur, or else calamity will happen. If Deutsche Bank went under, the German economy—and with it, all European economies— would collapse; and therefore, it's not a question of choice. Obviously, to just put out more bail-out packages per se, as the ECB and the EU Commission have done in the past, is completely useless because it makes the problem worse. Right now, it has reached the limit; because after helicopter money, what else do you expect to do?

It is not a choice; it is a life and death question, not only for Germany, but really for the entire trans-Atlantic sector.

Herrhausen and LaRouche

Ogden: Now, you have emphasized that the circumstances around the assassination of Alfred Herrhausen continue to be a crime about which the truth has not yet been fully told. It's something that in the United States, we can relate to the assassination of John F. Kennedy, in terms of the magnitude of what this meant for the turning point in the policy of Germany at that time. Obviously, it was in the context of the collapse of the Berlin Wall in the beginning of November 1989, and just less than one month later, at the very end of November, November 30th, that Herrhausen was assassinated in a very sophisticated attack on his convoy as he was travelling from his home to the Deutsche Bank headquarters. Helga, in an article that you wrote in 1992 titled, "New Evidence Emerges in the Herrhausen Assassination Case," you said:

"The key to the motive behind Herrhausen's assassination lies in 11 pages of a speech he was to deliver in the United States only four days after he was ambushed. The speech contained Herrhausen's vision of a new kind of relationship between eastern and western Europe, which would have fundamentally altered the world's future course."

And then you have a quotation from the speech, which I think is shocking when we go back and read that today, in consideration of what Mr. LaRouche and you were also both advocating for at that time. What he said, or what he was to say, in that speech that was never delivered, was the following:

"There should be assurances that the new credit will flow into specific, promising projects. It is therefore advisable that the export guarantees which the German Federal government wants to expand, be tied primarily to specific projects. In this connection, at this year's annual meeting of the IMF and World Bank in Washington, I proposed setting up a development bank on the spot; i.e., in Warsaw. Its task would be to bundle the aid and to channel it according to strict efficiency criteria. My vision is that such an institution could function somewhat like the Deutsche Kreditanstalt für Wiederaufbau, which traces its origins back to the Marshall Plan."

So, when you compare that speech that Herrhausen was about to give four days after he was assassinated, to what Lyn said in his speech in West Germany at the Kempinski Hotel in 1988, when he forecast the reunification of Germany and the collapse of the Berlin Wall, he said:

"Let us say that the United States and western Europe will cooperate to accomplish the successful rebuilding of the economy of Poland. There will be interference in the political system of government, but only a kind of Marshall Plan aid to rebuild Poland's industry and agriculture. If Germany agrees to this, let a process aimed at the reunification of the economies of Germany begin; and let this be the *punctum saliens* for western cooperation in assisting in the rebuilding of the economy of Poland."

EIRNS/Dean Andromidas

Lyndon H. LaRouche, Jr. addressing a press conference at the Kempinski Hotel in West Berlin, Oct. 22, 1988.

So, I think in the context of this speech that Herrhausen was about to deliver in New York, his cooperation with Helmut Kohl in terms of the reunification of Germany; and also the fact that he was on record calling for the debt relief—at least a partial debt relief, if not a full debt forgiveness of the Third World countries. He had met with the President of Mexico in 1987; he had surprised the world by delivering a speech at the World Bank in 1987 calling for the forgiveness of the debt of the Third World. All of these are right in parallel with what you and Lyn were advocating, going all the way back to 1975, back to the Operation Juarez and also with this Marshall Plan Productive Triangle proposal at the fall of the Berlin Wall. So, I think that certainly puts his assassination in the correct context to understand *cui bono*. Who benefitted from the fact that he was killed?

Unification: The Real Story

Zepp-LaRouche: Well, I think I would like to take it back a little bit, because this is not just a question of a murder which occurred 27 years ago. I want to recall what the period was, because most people have forgotten that Germany was not always unified; that the Berlin Wall came down. But this was one of the most dramatic developments in the post-war period. You remember that you had the peaceful demonstrations in the GDR [East Germany], the Monday demonstrations; the

German Chancellor Helmut Kohl in 1990.

Bundesarchiv

assure you, not even the German government had any idea that unification could be close; even if that was the primary political goal of the entire post-war period. Then the wall came down; and in the official documents which the German government published ten years later, they admitted they had no contingency plan for the case of German unification. Can you imagine that? The policy goal number one was to have German unification; and they had no plan. But we did have a plan.

So, then developments became extremely dramatic. On the 28th of November, Helmut Kohl probably took the most important step in his entire political career by putting forward the 10-point program. This was not yet a program for German unification, but it was a medium-term plan for the moving closer together of the two German states; the West German and East German states in a federation. But he did that without consulting the Allies, and he did it without even consulting his Liberal coalition partner, Mr. Genscher; but it was a first baby step in the direction of true German sovereignty. We know now that French President François Mitterrand gave an ultimatum to Kohl and said, either you give up the German D-mark and allow it to be replaced by a European common currency—what became the euro—or we will not agree to German unification.

Warsaw Pact still existed, and it was not clear what would happen. Would this lead to another 1956 like in Hungary, or a new Prague Spring, where Russian or Soviet tanks would come? Then the wall came down, and Mr. La-Rouche had this idea about German unification which you referenced, which he had presented in the Kempinski Hotel in 1988; so we had a plan. We put out immediately this proposal that German unification

Alfred Herrhausen (left), Chairman of Germany's largest commercial bank, Deutsche Bank, greets German Chancellor Helmut Kohl.

would have a mission; to have the Productive Triangle: to take the region from Paris, Berlin, Vienna — the economic powerhouse of the world at that time—and develop corridors into eastern Europe to transform Europe. We were the only ones who had any idea, because we were the only ones who even had an inkling that the Soviet Union would collapse, which Mr. LaRouche had already forecast in 1984. He said, if the Soviet Union sticks to their military policy of the Ogarkov plan,—which was basically the idea of gaining world dominance,— then they will collapse in five years. And I can

Two days after Kohl had put out this 10-point program, Herrhausen was assassinated. Everybody in the German elite at that point—and we talked to many people at that time—said this is not just an assassination, but since Herrhausen was the closest advisor to Kohl, this was a message to Kohl: Don't stick your neck out; do not dare to pursue and assert sovereignty. Be-

EIRNS/Stuart Lewis

President George W. Bush's security advisor Brent Scowcroft, a proponent of containing Germany, at a Nov. 28, 1988 conference of the Netherlands Atlantic Commission and the Institute for Foreign Policy Analysis.

his life. The circumstances were such that Kohl knew that the euro wouldn't work, and he said this is against German interests. He knew absolutely that you cannot have a European common currency without political union. So, he knew it wouldn't work; he knew it was against German interests. But he was forced by the circumstances to accept it, because you had Bush Sr., who had the policy of containment of Germany in the EU. It is well-established that originally Bush was against German unification, and he only went along with it because more experienced political advisors like Brent Scowcroft told him that if you oppose German unification, then the United States will lose all influence in Europe,— so we have to agree to it. But let's make sure Germany is contained. And that is what led to the infamous EU Maastricht agreement, which was the beginning of turning the EU into an imperial adjunct of the Anglo-American system. Helmut Schmidt, the late German Chancellor, in an equally surprising interview recently, before he died, said the whole Ukraine crisis,— which is right now what could be the trigger point for a war with Russia,— really started with the Maastricht agreement, because this is when the EU decided to do exactly what NATO has been doing ever since. Namely, to go for an eastward expansion, and move the EU

cause Germany in the entire post-war period was an occupied country; and at that time the saying went, "The best-kept public secret of NATO is that Germany is an occupied country and will remain an occupied country." So this tiny baby step in the direction of sovereignty by Kohl with the 10-point program, was obviously a contributing factor to why this assassination occurred. As you said, if Herrhausen had made this speech in New York the following week, you would have had a proposal coming from the leading banker which was practically in principle identical to what Mr. LaRouche and I proposed at the time; namely, that a unified Germany should take Poland as an example for the economic transformation of all the other countries of the Comecon.

Bundesarchiv

Chancellor of the Federal Republic of Germany Helmut Schmidt, shown in 1976.

and NATO just up to the borders of Russia.

So, the decision which was made in these really dramatic weeks and months, set the course. If Herrhausen had been alive and advised Kohl, conceptions like ours could have been implemented, and history would not be at the point where we are now. So the Herrhausen assassination not only meant the lost chance of 1989; everybody agreed at that time this was an historic chance that happens at best once a century. I called it the *Sternstunde* of Germany [literally "star hour," a dramatically compressed, fateful moment], because if you had a uni-

Then naturally, everything went haywire. At the EU summit which followed at the beginning of December in Strasbourg, everyone started to attack Kohl. In an interview later, he said these were the darkest hours of

fied Germany developing a peace plan for the 21st Century together with Russia, the whole world would look completely different. But as I said, all the successors of Herrhausen went in the direction of high-risk speculation, globalization, money for money's sake, the rich become richer, the poor become poorer, and all the problems we have today. All the problems we have today are not just caused by this one assassination, but the assassination is symptomatic for the paradigm shift to the worse.

It's a murder which has gone unpunished. The so-called murderers, the third generation of the Red Army Faction, probably never existed. There was even in the first German TV channel a documentary which said there has never been any evidence that any of the persons who supposedly were the murderers, ever really existed. So, the *cui bono*—well, it's the financial oligarchy which profited. And it really has the smell of something quite different—of an intelligence operation—as many of the leading figures who did not fit the Yalta norm were assassinated. But with the Herrhausen case, as you said, for Germany this is as important in terms of paradigm shift as the assassination was of John F. Kennedy.

And right now, when the entire banking system is absolutely at the verge of collapse, it is the last moment to do justice and really go back to the policies of Herrhausen. Even so, almost nobody knows any longer what real industrial banking is, because they are so money-greedy and absolutely suckers for the latest profit, that it would be a real uphill battle. But that battle must be fought if Europe and Germany and the rest of the trans-Atlantic sector are to survive; and probably beyond that, much of the world.

Ben Deniston: I think just looking at this transition period, I know that you and Mr. LaRouche had both made a warning that I think is very appropriate just to state in this context, that around the fall of the wall, this lost chance of '89, you had explicitly said to the world, if we attempt to replace this bankrupt, collapsing Soviet system with an equally bankrupt trans-Atlantic system, you're going to head to a collapse that's worse than what's happening now. But it seems like that really bridges this whole process from '89 to what we're seeing today as the culmination, the expression of what you warned of at that time. I think a challenge we have is to get across, is the importance of acting now on the level needed to make this shift we're talking about. What Lyn has laid out with this reform program for

Deutsche Bank is the beginning of this new paradigm. I think it's important to see it as an intervention in this whole collapse process you both had warned about, and forecast that this would be the consequence of failing to act then. That should help us understand how important it is to act now while we still have the chance.

There Is a Higher Power

Zepp-LaRouche: I remember that at that time, you had the problem of the Bush administration, Margaret Thatcher, François Mitterrand, who absolutely really ganged up to prevent Germany from assuming any such role of having an independent policy; especially in respect to Russia. They were always saying, "Oh, the West has won over communism." The only other person outside of us who totally contradicted them was John Paul II, the Pope of the time; who said, the people who now are triumphant and say the market economy is winning over communism, are absolutely wrong. If you don't believe it, look at the condition of the Third World, to see that the West has not won; because the moral condition of the developing countries speaks to the contrary.

Naturally, that is all the more true today, because if you look at the inhuman treatment of the refugee crisis, for example—they are still coming by the hundreds, every week by the thousands, over the Mediterranean; drowning. Even more are starving and dying of thirst and lack of water trying to cross the Sahara. That is also the condition of this system. The system is what causes all of this. Therefore, it is absolutely high time that we come to the question of how can we—as a human civilization—give ourselves an economy and a financial system which is adequate to human beings. And I think it's very important that we go back to the question of what is actually the creation of wealth. Is it what Margaret Thatcher said, is it the ability to buy cheap and sell dear,—the famous saying of Margaret Thatcher the greengrocer's daughter? Or is it the possession of raw materials? Or is it the control of the financial system? No; it's not. The only source of wealth is the creative power of the human being; and when that creative power is applied, then you have scientific and technological progress. That then leads to an increase of productivity in the economy.

That has been the battle between the American Revolution and the British Empire; between the free-traders and people like Alexander Hamilton who insisted that it is the creative power of labor which causes the well-being and the living standard and the longevity of

Lithograph of Friedrich List, 1838.

Otto von Bismarck, the first chancellor of united Germany.

the people. That was the philosophy of Friedrich List, the great German economist, who is now the most famous economist in China, by the way. That was the policy of Friedrich List and Henry C. Carey, the advisor of Lincoln, who both advised Bismarck through such people as Wilhelm von Kardoff, who was the head of the German industrialists' association in the time of Bismarck, and who changed the mind of Bismarck from being a free-trader into being an absolute believer in a protectionist system and in the idea that you have to further the productivity and creativity of your own population as the only source of wealth.

Wilhelm von Kardoff, in 1903.

Dr. Wilhelm Lautenbach

So, there is a lot of history involved; and what we are really talking about is taking Germany back to the ideas of Bismarck, of Friedrich List, of Henry C. Carey, and of Dr. Wilhelm Lautenbach, who in 1932 presented a plan to the Friedrich List Organization in Germany which was identical with what Roosevelt later proposed with the New Deal and the Reconstruction Finance Corporation, Glass-Steagall, and Bretton Woods. That was all in these proposals by Dr. Wilhelm Lautenbach, which, as history knows, unfortunately were not taken up; but instead you had Hjalmar Schacht, you had Hitler, you had before Mussolini, Franco, Petain, and you are in bed with fascists.

The question today is, can we, in time, go back to those conceptions which have proven to be productive and valuable for the economy; or do we plunge into a catastrophe of new fascism and new wars? So, on this question of Deutsche Bank, most people are so much in the day-to-day routine of making money, profits, and balance sheets,—and have dollar-bills coming out of their eyes,— that they have forgotten that there is something much more important about human life. And that is the happiness of people; the common good of people.

That's the reason why, in this call to honor the memory of Herrhausen,—using this crisis of Deutsche Bank now as a real paradigm shift to go back to these policies,— why I mentioned the great poem by Friedrich Schiller "The Cranes of Ibykus." And by the way, I would really urge our audience right now, who probably are not familiar with that poem: we have a translation which we can put on the website so it's easily accessible. But this poem is so powerful; it's written by Friedrich Schiller. It discusses not only the murder of the beloved poet Ibykus, but more important even, it discusses the power of nemesis, the power of natural law, which is a power which works in reality. It's not that God punishes every little thief who steals something by immediately chopping off his hand, but it is a power which revenges great injustice. And this poem discusses this in

An engraving of the Cranes of Ibykus, with the Erinyes in the foreground.

nucius.org

power through the prism of the poem. It's a very, very powerful way of reminding people that there is a higher power than what people think when they read the daily newspaper. So, please make the effort. Read it in English if you have to, but read it in German because there is another dimension to history than what people think. But only if you bring this forward, this inner strength, this inner power which people have almost lost in the trans-Atlantic sector, because people feel small, they feel impotent, they feel helpless. But what we have to unleash is exactly this inner strength so that people really become truly human again, and take history and destiny in their own hands. And that's exactly what the message is of Friedrich Schiller; who always thought that man is greater than his destiny, by resorting to these kinds of inner powers and higher authorities than the laws of money.

I think that having said that, I want to come back to the absolute need to find a handle, because right now the problem is, nobody has a handle on how to intervene with this financial crisis. And if the proposal of Mr. LaRouche is taken seriously, you have a way of dealing with the consequences, while avoiding the dangers of an uncontrollable collapse. You have to untangle this; you have to shut down this derivative system; you have to shut down the bubble. You have to do it in an orderly manner, because there's no point to merely a say let's just close it down or tax it or whatever. You have to find a skilled level of how you take over management of a bank—in this case, the Deutsche Bank; you have to put in a supervisory management committee which has to evaluate the validity and integrity of the outstanding obligations. Many of the derivatives have much more than two parties; they have two, three, four, and more parties. You have to untangle that. You probably have to write down the nominal value of these outstanding obligations. That way, you can put in a new basis, a new business plan for the bank which is in cohesion with the idea of credit policy in general. But you have to start to do that somewhere. The Herrhausen history and tradition is exactly what makes it very practical. We are not proposing something completely outlandish, utopian; this was the policy of Deutsche Bank at one point.

So therefore, I want to bring it back to this point; and

a very beautiful way by resorting to the Greek nemesis, the idea which was used in great Greek dramas to demonstrate this principle of the Erinyes. That there is this power that revenges this murder and other injustices; that there is a higher power than the arbitrariness of people's will. The poem is very, very powerful.

As a matter of fact, I would even urge you to learn German, just to read and understand that poem; because it teaches something about history. I think right now the Erinyes, those goddesses of revenge whom Friedrich Schiller has in this poem marching in the amphitheater—in circles—are bringing forward this higher

I would really urge all the people who are watching to make sure this proposal is distributed to all institutions which have anything to do with the economy, with industry, with people in political positions who should take care of the common good. And make sure that we get a serious debate. I know that in both election platforms of the Democratic Party and the Republican Party, you have the Glass-Steagall law in the platform. Now that is very good; we will have the conventions in the next weeks. This is not necessarily the stated position of the candidates; but it is in the platform.

So there is hope that if we mobilize in the right way, this change can occur before it's too late. But it's really one second, or maybe a nanosecond before midnight; so it's not a time for complacency. It's a time for action. Therefore, I would really urge you to join us; because we have a beautiful future ahead of us if we do the right thing. If we miss this moment, it can be the end of civilization; because the war danger is very real, not only in respect to NATO against Russia, but also the escalation around the South China Sea. We are not in a political void, but we are in one of these moments in history where a lot depends on the individual courage and the individual action. Therefore, I really ask you to join us to bring history in a better direction.

Ogden: Would you like to make any final remarks before we close?

Zepp-LaRouche: I would like to express my hope that enough people recognize that we have now reached a point where history will either be a total catastrophe—and most people are already thinking that; the people who are not completely dead because of drugs or other problems, they know that we are in a really unprecedented civilizational crisis. Even worse than any of the prewar situations of the 20th Century.

Just yesterday, one of the key advisers of the Kremlin said all the signs are of a prewar period; and that's true. We are in a prewar period; and unless we remove the real reason for the dynamic for war, which is the danger of a collapse of the trans-Atlantic financial system,— unless we remedy that, I'm almost certain that war will happen; and if that war happens, it's the logic of war that in that case all weapons available will be used. In the case of thermonuclear weapons, that would be it; there probably would not be anybody to even record what happened, because it would be the elimination of civilization. And therefore, the remedy for the financial crisis is not just a banking-technical affair; it really is the question of putting society back on a course where we all can survive as a human civilization. In a certain sense, it's what *The Federalist Papers* discussed. Can we give ourselves a political order which is suitable for man to organize his own affairs and govern according to the common good? So, it's a much larger issue; and I'm very optimistic that it can be done. But it requires an extraordinary effort, and it requires all of you.

DOCUMENTATION

The Strategic Vision and Lost Opportunities of 1989

July 19—On October 12, 1988, Lyndon LaRouche delivered an historic presentation at West Berlin's Kempinski Hotel, in which he proposed a pathway towards the peaceful integration of the Warsaw Pact into the world economy, by means of West German economic assistance to Poland. In that address, before media, LaRouche first proposed that German reunification was both possible and imminent.

One year later, Alfred Herrhausen, the Chairman of Deutsche Bank and a top economic policy adviser and personal friend of then German Chancellor Helmut Kohl, planned to present a similar vision of cooperation with the soon-to-be liberated nations of Eastern Europe. His scheduled Arthur Burns Lecture in New York City was never delivered, because he was assassinated four days before on Nov. 30, 1989.

The text of Herrhausen's scheduled speech was published in the *New York Times,* but the full import of the Herrhausen assassination was suppressed, and the actual authors of his murder were never caught or prosecuted.

Instead, his murder was blamed on a non-existent "Third Generation" Red Army Faction (RAF). The day that Herrhausen was scheduled to be in New York City to deliver that lecture, French President Mitterrand delivered an ultimatum to Chancellor Kohl, on behalf of both France and Great Britain: Germany would acquiesce in a European single-currency regime that would prove, over time, to be a straight-jacket against Germany's economic progress and against the Herrhausen plans for Germany to take the lead in integrating the nations of the former Warsaw Pact, including the former Soviet Union, into an integrated Eurasian economic sphere.

Although the Kohl government ultimately capitulated to the threats from Mitterrand and British Prime Minister Thatcher, leading to the 1992 Maastricht Treaty, the LaRouche movement went on to propose an elaboration of the concepts spelled out by Lyndon La-Rouche and Alfred Herrhausen, in what came to be known as the European Productive Triangle. That proposal, first issued in Aug. 1990, even before the full collapse of the Soviet Union, was later expanded into the Eurasian Landbridge plan, that extended the Eurasian integration from the Atlantic coasts of Western Europe to the Pacific coasts of China. Today, the Chinese government has adopted that larger Eurasian Landbridge vision into President Xi Jinping's One Belt, One Road program.

Below are two critical documents of that sweep of events from the late 1980s into the early 1990s. The Herrhausen assassination, and the frame-up jailing of Lyndon LaRouche by a corrupt George H.W. Bush Administration in Jan. 1989, altered the course of history, leading to what Helga Zepp-LaRouche called the "lost opportunity of 1989."

'MARSHALL PLAN' FOR POLAND

U.S. Policy Toward the Reunification of Germany

by Lyndon H. LaRouche, Jr.

Printed below is the Oct. 12, 1988 press conference statement by Lyndon LaRouche at the Kempinski Hotel, West Berlin, Federal Republic of Germany, a year before the events that led to the reunification of East and West Germany. In his presentation, LaRouche stated that Germany could be reunified in the process of playing a key role to solve the food emergencies in Poland and other eastern European countries that were in an economic crisis.

I am here today, to report to you on the subject of U.S. policy for the prospects of reunification of Germany. What I present to you now, will be a featured topic in a half-hour U.S. television broadcast, nationwide, prior to next month's presidential election. I could think of no more appropriate place to unveil this new proposal, than here in Berlin.

I am the third of the leading candidates for election as the next President of the United States. Although I shall not win that election, my campaign will almost certainly have a significant influence in shaping some of the policies of the next President.

Although we can not know with certainty who will be the winner of a close contest between Vice President George Bush and Massachusetts Gov. Michael Dukakis, it is the best estimate in the United States today, that Mr. Bush will win the largest electoral vote. Obviously, I am not supporting Mr. Bush's candidacy, and I am not what is called a "spoiler" candidate, working secretly on Mr. Bush's behalf. Nonetheless, should Mr. Bush win, it would be likely that I would have some significant, if indirect influence on certain of the policies of the next administration. How this result would affect the destiny of Germany and Central Europe generally, is the subject of my report here today.

By profession, I am an economist in the tradition of Gottfried Wilhelm Leibniz and Friedrich List in Germany, and of Alexander Hamilton and Mathew and Henry Carey in the United States. My political principles are those of Leibniz, List, and Hamilton, and are also consistent with those of Friedrich Schiller and Wilhelm von Humboldt. Like the founders of my republic, I have an uncompromising belief in the principle of absolutely sovereign nation-states, and I am therefore opposed to all supranational authorities which might undermine the sovereignty of any nation. However, like Schiller, I believe that every person who aspires to become a beautiful soul, must be at the same time a true patriot of his own nation, and also a world-citizen.

For these reasons, during the past fifteen years I have become a specialist in my country's foreign affairs. As a result of this work, I have gained increasing, significant influence among some circles around my own government on the interrelated subjects of U.S. foreign policy and strategy. My role during 1982 and 1983 in working with the U.S. National Security Council to shape the adoption of the policy known as the Strategic Defense Initiative, or SDI, is an example of this. Although the details are confidential, I can report to you that my views on the current strategic situation are more influential in the United States today than at any time during the past.

Therefore, I can assure you that what I present to you now, on the subject of prospects for the reunification of Germany, is a proposal which will be studied most seriously among the relevant establishment circles inside the United States.

Under the proper conditions, many today will agree, that the time has come for early steps toward the reunification of Germany, with the obvious prospect that Berlin might resume its role as the capital.

For the United States, for Germans, and for Europe generally, the question is, will this be brought about by assimilating the Federal Republic of Germany and West Berlin into the East bloc's economic sphere of influence, or can it be arranged differently? In other words,

CC/Lear 21

Demonstrators on the Berlin Wall in 1989, demanding that it be opened. It was opened, Nov. 9, 1989.

is a united Germany to become part of a Europe from the Atlantic to the Urals, as President de Gaulle proposed, or, as Mr. Gorbachov desires, a Europe from the Urals to the Atlantic?

The Reality of the Worldwide Food Crisis

I see a possibility, that the process of reunification could develop as de Gaulle proposed. I base this possibility upon the reality of a terrible worldwide food crisis which has erupted during the past several months, and will dominate the world's politics for at least two years to come.

The economy of the Soviet bloc is a terrible, and worsening failure. In Western European culture, we have demonstrated that the successes of nations of big industries depend upon the technologically progressive independent farmer, and what you call in Germany the *Mittelstand* [Germany's small and medium-sized entrepreneurs]. Soviet culture in its present form is not capable of applying this lesson. Despite all attempts at structural reforms, and despite any amount of credits supplied from the West, the Soviet bloc economy as a whole has reached the critical point, that, in its present form, it will continue to slide downhill from here on, even if the present worldwide food crisis had not erupted.

I do not foresee the possibility of genuine peace between the United States and Soviet Union earlier than thirty or forty years still to come. The best we can do in the name of peace, is to avoid a new general war between the powers. This war-avoidance must be based partly on our armed strength, and our political will. It must be based also, on rebuilding the strength of our economies.

At the same time that we discourage Moscow from dangerous military and similar adventures, we must heed the lesson taught us by a great military scientist nearly four centuries ago, Niccolò Macchiavelli: we must also provide an adversary with a safe route of escape. We must rebuild our economies to the level at which we can provide the nations of the Soviet bloc an escape from the terrible effects of their economic suffering.

I give a concrete example.

Recently, in response to the food crisis, I sponsored the formation of an international association, called Food For Peace. This association has just recently held its founding conference in Chicago Sept. 3-4, and since then has been growing rapidly inside the United States and in other nations represented by delegates attending that conference.

One of the points I have stressed, in supporting this Food For Peace effort, is that the Soviet bloc will require the import of about 80 million tons of grain next year, as a bare minimum for the pressing needs of its population. China is experiencing a terrible food crisis, too. As of now, the food reserves are exhausted. There are no more food reserves in the United States, and the actions of the European Commission in Brussels have brought the food reserves of Western Europe to very low levels. Next year, the United States and Western Europe will be cut off from the large and growing amount of food imports during recent years, because of the collapse of food production in developing nations throughout most of the world.

During 1988, the world will have produced between 1.6 and 1.7 billion tons of grains, already a disastrous shortage. To ensure conditions of political, and strategic stability during 1989 and 1990, we shall require approximately 2.4 to 2.5 billion tons of grain each year. At those levels, we would be able to meet minimal Soviet needs; without something approaching those levels, we could not.

If the nations of the West would adopt an emergency agricultural policy, those nations, working together, could ensure that we reach the level of food supply corresponding to about 2.4 billion tons of grains. It would be a major effort, and would mean scrapping the present agricultural policies of many governments and supranational institutions, but it could be accomplished. If we are serious about avoiding the danger of war during the coming two years, we will do just that.

By adopting these kinds of policies, in food supplies and other crucial economic matters, the West can foster the kind of conditions under which the desirable approach to reunification of Germany can proceed on the basis a majority of Germans on both sides of the Wall desire it should. I propose that the next government of the United States should adopt that as part of its foreign policy toward Central Europe.

Rebuild the Economies of Eastern Europe

I shall propose the following concrete perspective to my government. We say to Moscow: We will help you. We shall act to establish Food For Peace agreements among the international community, with the included goal that neither the people of the Soviet bloc nor developing nations shall go hungry. In response to our good faith in doing that for you, let us do something which will set an example of what can be done to help solve the economic crisis throughout the Soviet bloc generally.

Let us say that the United States and Western Europe will cooperate to accomplish the successful rebuilding of the economy of Poland. There will be no interference in the political system of government, but only a kind of Marshall Plan aid to rebuild Poland's industry and agriculture. If Germany agrees to this, let a process aimed at the reunification of the economies of Germany begin, and let this be the *punctum saliens* for Western cooperation in assisting the rebuilding of the economy of Poland.

We, in the United States and Germany, should say to the Soviet bloc, let us show what we can do for the peoples of Eastern Europe, by this test, which costs you really nothing. Then, you judge by the results, whether this is a lesson you wish to try in other cases.

I am now approaching the conclusion of my report. I have two more points to identify.

All of us who are members of that stratum called world-class politicians, know that the world has now entered into what most agree is the end of an era. The state of the world as we have known it during the postwar period is ended. The only question is, whether the new era will be better or worse than the era we are now departing?

The next two years, especially, will be the most dangerous period in modern European history, and that worldwide. Already, in Africa, entire nations, such as Uganda, are in the process of vanishing from the map, biologically. Madness on a mass scale, of a sort which Central Europe has not known since the New Dark Age of the Fourteenth Century, has already destroyed Cambodia, is threatening to take over the Middle East as a whole, and is on the march, to one degree or another, in every part of the world. As a result of these conditions of crisis, the world has never been closer to a new world war than the conditions which threaten us during the next four years ahead. What governments do during the coming two years will decide the fate of all humanity for a century or more to come.

There have been similar, if not identical periods of crisis in history before this, but, never, to our best knowledge, on a global scale, all at once.

I recall the famous case of a certain German gentleman of the Weimar period. This gentleman was persuaded that a second world war was inevitable. He searched the world for a place to which he might move his family, to be out of the areas in which the next war would be fought. So, when the war erupted, he and his family were living in the remote Solomon Islands, on the island of Guadalcanal.

In this period of crisis, there is no place in which any man or woman can safely hide in a crisis-ridden world without food. One can not duck politics, with the idea of taking care of one's career and family, until this storm blows over. There is no place, for any man or woman to hide. There is no room for today's political pragmatists in the leadership of governments now. If we are to survive, we must make boldly imaginative decisions, on the condition that they are good choices, as well as bold ones.

The time has come for a bold decision on U.S. policy toward Central Europe.

If there is no Soviet representative here in this audience at the moment, we may be certain that the entire content of my report to you now will be in Moscow, and will be examined at high levels there, before many hours have passed. The Soviet leadership has said in its newspapers and elsewhere, many times, that it consid-

ers me its leading adversary among leading individual public figures today. Nonetheless, Moscow regards me with a curious sort of fascination, and, since President Reagan first announced the Strategic Defense Initiative, considers everything I say on policy matters to be influential, and very credible.

Moscow will read the report I deliver here today. It will wait, as Soviet political leaders do, to see what other circles around the U.S. establishment and government might echo the kind of proposal I have identified. Once they see such a signal from those quarters, Moscow will treat my proposal very seriously, and will begin exploring U.S. and European thinking on this.

Germany's Sovereign Choice

As far as I am concerned, it is Germans who must make the sovereign decision on their choice of fate for their nation. My function is to expand the range of choices available to them. So, I have come to Berlin, where the delivery of this report will have the maximum impact in Moscow, as well as other places.

I conclude my remarks with the following observation.

Moscow hates me, but in their peculiar way, the Soviets trust me to act on my word. Moscow will believe, quite rightly, that my intentions toward them are exactly what I described to you today. I would therefore hope, that what I am setting into motion here today, will be a helpful contribution to establishing Germany's sovereign right to choose its own destiny.

For reasons you can readily recognize from the evidence in view, I know my German friends and acquaintances rather well, and share the passions of those who think of Germany with loving memory of Leibniz, Schiller, Beethoven, Humboldt, and that great statesman of freedom, Freiherr vom Stein. If I can not predict Germany's decisions in this matter exactly, I believe that if what I have set afoot here today is brought to success, the included result will be that the Reichstag building over there, will be the seat of Germany's future parliament, and the beautiful Charlottenburger Schloss, the future seat of government.

If the conditions arise, in which that occurs, President de Gaulle's dream of a Europe from the Atlantic to the Urals will be the peaceful outcome of thirty years or so of patient statecraft, and that durable peace will come to Europe and the world within the lifetime of those graduating from universities today.

Heute, bin ich auch ein Berliner.

New Horizons in Europe

Printed below is an excerpt from Alfred Herrhausen's prepared speech which was to have been delivered in New York City, Dec. 4, 1989, four days after his assassination on Nov. 30, 1989.

Let me expand a little on the specific case of Poland. In addition to the patent shortcomings in the way its domestic economy is organized, Poland is also grappling with an exceptionally large external debt of almost $40 billion. For domestic reforms to have at least a chance of success, the debt problem needs to be solved promptly. In the past, the banks have agreed to regular reschedulings, but now the onus is on government lenders assembled in the Paris Club to come up with a helpful contribution. They account for roughly two-thirds of the country's external debt. If there is to be a permanent solution, this will require enlarging the strategies hitherto adopted to include a reduction of debt or debt service. However, such support can only make a mean-

ingful contribution to reform policy if it is used sensibly and efficiently, as was the case with the Marshall Plan funds in shattered postwar Western Europe .

But this—vital—precondition still has to be fulfilled, given the dominant role of the state sector whose bureaucratic structures have remained largely intact so far. What, then, is to be done? The indispensable aid from outside should, I feel, be supplemented by a temporary scheme whereby external donors also have a say in the application of funds provided. The task here is to ensure that new loans are channelled into promising projects. It is, therefore, to be commended that the export credit guarantees which the West German government is prepared to extend are largely project-oriented. In fact, it was a *Polish* idea, that a committee of experts drawn from both countries evaluate likely projects in order to make sure that the costly mistakes of the seventies are avoided.

In this context, I proposed—on the occasion of this year's Annual Meeting of the World Bank and the IMF in Washington—the establishment of a development bank on the spot, that is in Warsaw. Its job would be to bundle incoming aid and deploy it in accordance with strict efficiency criteria. I could well imagine that such an institution might be set up along the lines of the German *Kreditanstalt für Wiederaufbau,* the Reconstruction Loan Corporation, whose origin goes back to the Marshall plan.

Representatives of the creditor countries should hold the majority in the management board of this new institution. Such a Polish "Institute for Economic Renewal" (IER), as it could be called, would have two functions: it should help and monitor. Since both these functions can only be exercised in close cooperation with the Polish authorities and with Polish trade and industry, genuine involvement on the part of the Institute in the Polish economy and the country's development process would be absolutely essential. It could be set up "until further notice" or come under Polish control after a transitional period. By channelling Western "help towards self-help" in the right directions, the Institute could play a constructive role in economic reform. [Atlantik-Brücke e.V., Rundschreiben Nr. 12/1989, pp. 7-9]

Restore Herrhausen's Deutsche Bank For Peace via Economic Development

by Kesha Rogers

Kesha Rogers in Houston, Texas, is a leader of the La-Rouche Political Action Committee and leads a campaign to revive the U.S. Space Program.

July 18—Lyndon LaRouche has now called for a one-time recapitalization of Deutsche Bank, on condition that the bank return to the tradition of its late Chairman, Alfred Herrhausen, a tradition of banking for industrial and human development, and not speculation. Herrhausen was assassinated at the time the Berlin Wall came down in 1989, because of his vision.

LaRouche's proposal, when combined with Russia's and China's standing invitation to Europe and the United States to join them in the New Silk Road programs of maritime, land, and space development, is the doorway through which Europe can escape the desolation and destruction of imminent bankruptcy and war, and enter into a new age of renaissance. The reorientation and recapitalization of Deutsche Bank will provide Europe the opportunity to take its proper place in implementing the world development paradigm of Lyndon and Helga LaRouche in their collaboration with the late Krafft Ehricke.

YouTube Screenshot/Deutschlandfunk
Alfred Herrhausen, chairman of Deutsche Bank, during an October 17, 1989 interview with German public radio, Deutschlandfunk.

The Potential of Europe

Europe once had—within living memory—the one of the densest networks of advanced machine tool design and scientific research in the world, typified by the small and medium-sized tool and die shops of the *Mittelstand*. This sector of the physical economy is the most efficient means by which new universal physical principles, as discovered through a robust human space exploration program, can be made widely available to society in the form of spin-off technologies. Deutsche Bank must be reoriented and recapitalized to provide the credit for the resurgence of this sector, so that Europe—as one Europe, from the Atlantic to the Urals, as President de Gaulle proposed—can be brought fully into collaboration with Asia, all the way to the Bering Strait, and with the World Land-Bridge.

It is man's destiny to undertake such exploration and colonization of space. In addition to other benefits obtained from space exploration, some of them incalculable, the mobilization of technological progress to accomplish this mission will ensure the highest potential rate of growth of the economy, per capita, on Earth.

Let us look back at the basis for this entry into what has been called the Age of Reason, as it was laid out by Ehricke and Lyndon LaRouche more than 30 years ago.

Ehricke envisioned regular transit to and from a permanent lunar scientific base, which he named Selenopolis. The establishment of permanent colonies on the Moon, and flourishing economic trade between the Moon and Earth, obviously requires immense advances in science and engineering. Both LaRouche and Ehricke emphasized the necessity of quickly harnessing thermonuclear fusion as a power source and for industrial processes such as the fusion torch. In Ehricke's 1972 paper, "Large Scale Processing of Lunar Materials," he describes a few of the new types of products that a lunar industrial base, would manufacture:

For the terrestrial markets, large quantities of electronic components, high-temperature alloys for improved thermal conversion equipment, ultra-hard alloys, special bearing alloys for transportation systems, foam metals, special alloys for seawater resistant structures, and brine resistant geothermal power equipment, to name only a few of the initial product lines; for the extraterrestrial market, large structures for lunar and circumlunar factories and dwelling units, for large structures in geosynchronous and even in near-Earth orbit.

Lyndon LaRouche recognized that Ehricke's proposed colonization of the Moon would lead to the colonization of Mars. In 1984, LaRouche laid out a Moon-Mars colonization program in which he pointed to four categories of technological advances needed for that program:

CC BY-SA 2.0

Computer-controlled spot welding in the BMW plant in Leipzig, Germany, 2005, using industrial robots manufactured by KUKA, an Augsburg firm.

• Controlled thermonuclear fusion for space propulsion, and related plasma technologies

• Means for producing coherent electromagnetic radiation of high energy-density cross section, and the development of new qualities of materials and production processes using these beams

• Optical biophysics as the basis for management of synthetic biospheres in interplanetary travel on spacecraft, and in controlled environments in colonies, including their production of food

• Advanced generations of computer systems designed for processing nonlinear functions implicit in a Gauss-Riemann electrodynamic manifold.

The Mission of a True Space Age

In a paper titled, "A Vision for Lunar Settlement," Ehricke wrote, "Our work in space will change Earth's present closed world environment into an open one, with access to vast space resources and other critically needed benefits that will greatly improve the lives of all people, and preserve Earth at its best—as man's home and garden for the maximum human future."

The full potential of a true space age must be brought about now. The mission of such a truly productive society is to give meaning to the lives of its citizens, so that children born today can grow up confident that they are taking part in contributing to a continuing, greater mission for all mankind. That is the potential that Deutsche Bank, reorganized for the purposes cherished by Alfred Herrhausen, and when combined with the New Silk Road, can unleash.

Ehricke's understanding of mankind's Extraterrestrial Imperative and Lyndon LaRouche's grasp of the science of physical economy both orient the economic and spiritual life of mankind around a principle of unlimited progress defined by advances in the cognitive and creative practice of humankind at large. Productivity is increased by transforming these discoveries into usable technologies, granting us access to a better life, with a fuller sense of meaning and connection to past and future generations. No other industrial, scientific, or cultural endeavor can so rapidly and so profoundly increase this rate of improvement in the human condition, as mankind's break-out into the Solar system.

If allowed to do so, Europe's renewed productive capabilities will become a powerful engine of progress for all humanity. European policy will shift toward a win-win approach with Russia and China, focussed on the common aims of mankind in the Solar system, instead of massing troops on its borders.

II. Can Nuclear War Be Averted?

SOUTH CHINA SEA

Behind the Phony Arbitration Ruling

by William Jones

July 16—A ruling on July 12 by an *ad hoc* arbitration panel, appointed by a Japanese judge under the Law of the Sea Convention, went well beyond its mandate in making a determination on the territorial disputes in the South China Sea between China and the Philippines, thereby pushing the region closer to military conflict between China and the United States. The July 12 ruling, if implemented, would effectively deprive China of territorial rights, recognized for centuries, over certain island chains in the South China Sea. While on the surface the decision appears to be a legitimate "court ruling," it is actually based on a "hidden agenda," as Chinese State Councilor Yang Jiechi noted in an interview with state media on July 14.

After reviewing in depth authoritative Chinese responses to this phony ruling, which are entirely justified as far as they go, we will conclude by referring to Lyndon LaRouche's record on the issue.

The arbitration was initiated by Philippine President Benigno Aquino III in 2013, in an attempt to obtain a ruling on the status of islands generally recognized as Chinese territorial islands in the South China Sea, but which lie in close proximity to the Philippine coast. They have, however, never been considered a part of Philippine territory in any of the treaties defining the Philippines as a nation.

While the dispute directly involves China and the Philippines, State Councilor Yang Jiechi, for many years China's Ambassador to the United States, clearly detects in the arbitration the long arm of the U.S. Administration, which is concerned about China's rapid development, economically and militarily, in the region and would who like to see China "contained." "The South China Sea arbitration has been a political farce all along," Yang told reporters in his interview, "staged

On May 26, 2015, President Vladimir Putin of Russia met with Chinese State Councilor Yang Jiechi at the Kremlin.

under the cover of law and driven by a hidden agenda." "Certain countries outside the region have attempted to deny China's sovereign rights and interests in the South China Sea through the arbitration," he said. "They have even brought other countries into the scheme to isolate and discredit China in the international community with a view to holding back China's peaceful development."

Instant Activation for the 'Award'

Just a few hours after the court had issued its "award," effectively declaring most of China's territorial claims in the South China Sea null and void, the Center for Strategic and International Studies held an all-day conference in Washington demanding that China abide by the ruling of this arbitration court.

Daniel Kritenbrink, the Asia Director of the U.S. National Security Council, speaking at the CSIS event, reiterated this demand. "The decision is final and legally binding," Kritenbrink said. "Stability derives from order and predictability. And order and predictability stem from all countries operating based on a common set of rules." He reiterated U.S. policy that there should be "freedom of navigation" for civilian *and* military ships and aircraft throughout the length of the South China Sea. Therefore, already on Day One, a campaign was begun to accuse China of being in violation of international law if it did not accept the rulings of this *ad hoc* tribunal and give up its territorial claims in the South China Sea.

But the Chinese side, which had continually called for resolving the maritime disputes with the Philippines in accordance with international law—that is, first and foremost through negotiations between the parties themselves—found this avenue thwarted by President Aquino's unwillingness to engage in talks. Arbitration, according to the UN Convention on the Law of the Seas (UNCLOS), remains an option if both parties conclude that the dispute cannot be settled through negotiation. That was not the case here. When Aquino announced that he was going to unilaterally request that the matter go to arbitration, China therefore formally withdrew from the case, which it had the right to do according to UNCLOS.

Given that state of affairs and the refusal of the Philippines to negotiate, it was surprising that the *ad hoc* arbitration court agreed to take the case at all. UNCLOS has no jurisdiction over territorial matters, as firmly stated in the preamble of the UNCLOS treaty, and this case clearly impinged on territorial disputes between China and the Philippines, thus providing a firm basis for the court to let the matter lie.

But nonetheless, the court took up the case and handed down a sweeping ruling which was a gross intrusion into a territorial dispute. By narrowing the definition of an "island" to a body of land having its own source of fresh water, the panel transformed the entire Nansha (Spratly) Island archipelago into a pile of rocks overnight, and thus not to be considered as territorial possessions. Some of these "rocks" then would became a part of the Philippine exclusive economic zone, as defined by UNCLOS as the surrounding waters measured out to 200 miles from the country's coastline.

State Councilor Yang Jiechi suspected that there was

South China Sea

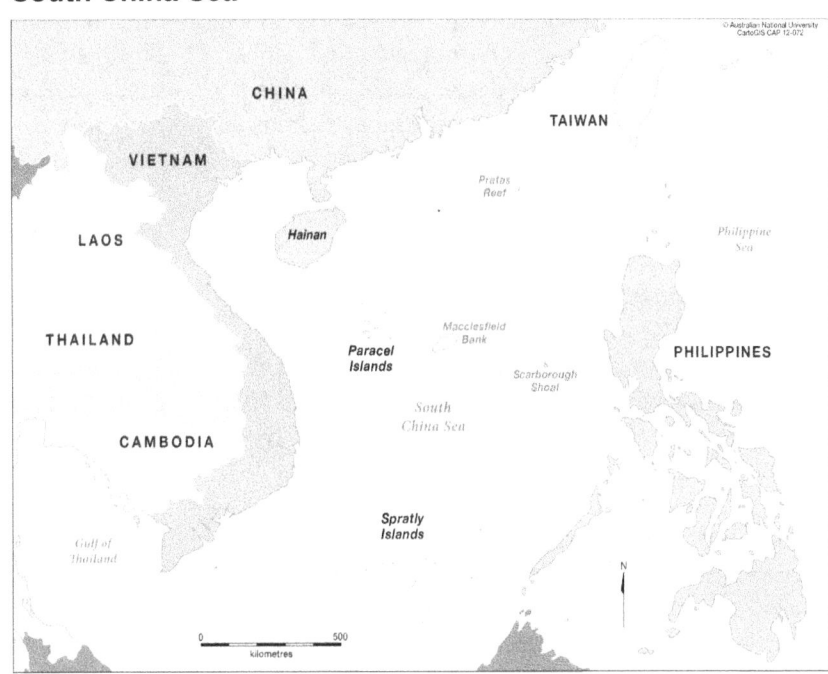

much more to this arbitration gambit than the somewhat erratic action of a somewhat unpredictable Philippine President, and that the "hidden agenda" of the U.S. Administration in its "pivot to Asia" played a major role in bringing it about. The reaction of the United States to the decision, as clearly indicated by Kritenbrink's comments, really corroborates that suspicion.

China's Historical Claims

The South China Sea is a relatively large body of water stretching around 1,200 miles north to south and 600 miles east to west. It is bordered by China, Malaysia, Indonesia, the Philippines, and Taiwan. China has utilized and administered four island groups in this sea for centuries, the most important of which are the Paracel Islands in the northern part of the sea, approximately 120 miles from China's Hainan Island, and the Spratly Islands, some 560 miles from China.

There is clear documentation that China discovered and began to name the Spratlys as early as the Han Dynasty (2nd Century B.C.) and have exercised jurisdiction over the islands at least since the Tang Dynasty (late 8th to early 9th century A.D.).

In 1933, the French, who then controlled Vietnam, occupied nine Nansha (Spratly) Islands, a move vociferously protested by the Republic of China, which took measures to beef up its own presence on the islands. The islands were occupied by the Japanese in World War II. In 1943, at the meeting in Cairo between President Franklin Roosevelt, Winston Churchill, and Chiang Kai-shek, the allies issued a declaration saying clearly that those islands still occupied by the Japanese must be returned to China after the war. This statement was reiterated after the death of Roosevelt by the Potsdam Declaration, signed by Truman, Churchill, and Stalin. And in 1946, officials from the Republic of China were brought by ship, with the blessing of the supreme commander, Douglas MacArthur, to reoccupy the islands.

The extensive documentation archived by China's National Institute for South China Sea Studies leaves little room for doubt about the legitimacy of China's territorial claims.

Rival Claims to Resources

China's territorial claims were also upheld in U.S. documents at the time, and no one, including the other countries in the region, contested them. And yet with the rapid development of offshore drilling in the 1970s, the resources of the South China Sea became more attractive. Some of the other coastal states, including Vietnam and the Philippines, then began to occupy some of the islands and reefs in each of the island chains, sometimes with troops. As this was changing the facts on the ground in areas China claimed as its territory, China began to follow suit and began its own program of construction on the islands.

When the UN Convention on the Law of the Seas was formulated in 1982, it established the concept of Exclusive Economic Zones (EEZs) to create a framework for resolving disputes over newly accessible maritime resources. The UNCLOS stipulates that each country has its recognized 12-mile maritime territorial border, measured from its coast, but also has the right to a 200-mile EEZ in which it has exclusive rights to utilize the maritime resources. In the South China Sea, this created overlapping claims for EEZs, which clearly impinged on China's territorial claims. This was the source of the maritime disputes. In the 1980s, China's paramount leader Deng Xiaoping proposed to the other nations that they shelve these disputes and begin to carry out joint development of the maritime resources of the region.

China subsequently signed agreements with the Philippines with regard to the South China Sea. In 1999 the two countries held the first China-Philippines Experts Group Meeting on Confidence-Building Measures, issuing a joint statement "that the dispute should be peacefully settled through consultation." In 2004, the China National Offshore Oil Corporation and the Philippine National Company signed the Agreement for Joint Marine Seismic Undertaking in Certain Areas in the South China Sea, and in 2005, national oil companies from China, the Philippines and Vietnam signed the Tripartite Agreement for Joint Seismic Undertaking in Certain Areas in the South Sea.

Largely due to foot-dragging by the Philippines, however, both of these undertakings have stalled. In 2000, after 26 years of negotiation, China settled with Vietnam the delimitation of territorial seas, EEZ, and continental shelf in Beibu Bay, which lies between Vietnam and China, and made arrangements for fishery cooperation.

In November 2002, China signed with ASEAN member states, which includes the Philippines, the Declaration on the Conduct of Parties in the South China Sea (DOC), which committed the signatories to resolve disputes through negotiation, to exercise restraint, and to refrain from carrying out activities that might complicate or escalate disputes and affect peace and stability. So with diplomacy moving forward on the issue of resource-sharing and a desire on the part of China to engage in negotiations on the issues of maritime delimitation, why did the Philippines in 2013 make the submission for arbitration?

Big Brother Steps In

Since the initiation of the "Asia Pivot" by the Obama Administration, the United States has expressed concern about losing its absolute predominance in the region. By tightening up its traditional Cold War alliances with Japan, South Korea, the Philippines, and Australia, sending half of the U.S. fleet to the Pacific to engage in "freedom of navigation" operations in the South China Sea, and contesting Chinese territorial claims, the U.S. has made it clear to China that the United States intends to "contain" its rise.

While China would like to engage the United States on an equal basis in the region and in the world at large, the U.S. still insists on maintaining the type of Pax Americana that characterized the world after the demise of the Soviet Union. And it is intent on maintaining its predominance at all costs. "We aren't going to let China make the rules," President Obama said, in relation to his nearly defunct Trans-Pacific Partnership trade proposal. This is the crux of the matter.

But given the ongoing collapse of the London-New

whitehouse.gov//Pete Souza

China's then Foreign Minister Yang Jiechi meeting President Obama at the White House in 2009.

York financial system, the "rules" governing the world today have serious flaws and have to be changed. As a responsible member of the international community, China desires—and deserves—a say in formulating the rules governing the world we live in. But the United States is not inclined to let that happen.

The reaction of the Chinese Government to the arbitration ruling has been swift and decisive. It will not accept the decision. The arbitration panel is not the International Court of Justice. It is not an arm of the United Nations, as the Secretary-General was keen on underlining after the decision was issued. And, China insists, the decision is not even consistent with the UNCLOS treaty under which such arbitration courts are allowed to be formed. China has received backing on that point from many nations and many noted legal scholars. And in this particular case, China notes, the decision to take the issue to arbitration was clearly made in bad faith.

Was it done in collusion with U.S. officials or individuals who wanted some decision unacceptable to China, in order to libel China as in violation of international law and to justify increased forays with heavily armed naval vessels on China's doorstep?

State Councilor Yang seems to think so. "Certain countries outside the region have attempted to deny China's sovereign rights and interests in the South China Sea through the arbitration," he said. "They have even brought other countries into the scheme to isolate and discredit China in the international community, with a view to holding back China's peaceful development."

But China is not going to cede any territory on the basis of a decision made by a court without proper jurisdiction, and which acted in "bad faith."

"Sovereignty is a bottom line for China," Yang said. "Big as China is, we cannot afford to give away a single inch of territory that our ancestors have left to us. China's territorial sovereignty and maritime rights and interests in the South China Sea have been formed over the course of over two thousand years. They are fully backed by historical and legal evidence. Under no circumstances can they ever be negated by a so-called award that is full of nonsense. The award can neither change historical facts nor deny China's claims of rights and interests in the South China Sea. Still less can it make us waver in our resolve and determination to safeguard territorial sovereignty and maritime rights and interests. China's position of not accepting or recognizing the award will not change."

Freedom of Navigation a Red Herring

The other aspect of the South China Sea has to do with China's ability to defend itself. The devastation wrought on China during the last 150 years by the Opium Wars and the Japanese invasion is seen as largely a result of China's lack of an effective navy. And China is determined that it will not happen again. It is building a strong navy, and its naval presence in the South China Sea and East China Sea is paramount and will increase until the tensions with the United States and Japan recede.

China has never threatened freedom of navigation and is totally at ease about, and supportive of, the smooth coming and going of commercial maritime traffic. It is something else with regard to the naval vessels of foreign powers, some with possible hostile intent toward China. U.S. "freedom of navigation" forays with destroyers or aircraft carriers are viewed quite differently than ordinary commercial traffic by naval analysts.

As Senior Colonel Zhou Bo, the director of the Chinese Ministry of Defense's Center for International Security Cooperation, told CCTV News in an interview

Britain's HMS Nemesis in 1841 destroys Chinese ships, during the Opium Wars; painting by Edward Duncan (1843).

on July 8: "We have never impeded freedom of navigation for commercial vessels. But we do not endorse American naval reconnaissance in the South China Sea because we don't consider that they're coming with an olive branch, but that they're breaking into my backyard and trying to read the pin number of the safe in my house. And they come here on a daily basis."

But this is exactly the reason for the U.S. Navy's stress on "innocent passage" for naval vessels in the region. The acceptance of Chinese territorial claims in the South China Sea would throw something of a monkey wrench into those close coastal reconnaissance operations, which are considered by the Pentagon as crucial for keeping China "boxed in." Bringing Australia and Japan into the region in an attempt to "internationalize" these operations will only add fuel to the fire.

The Ball Is Now in Duterte's Court

The ruling of the arbitration panel has garnered a great deal of criticism from many nations and legal experts. Taiwan, which is also in possession of some of the islands as a result of the post-war agreements, also protested the decision. In an ironic twist, the newly elected leader of Taiwan, the head of a pro-independence party, has sent ships to Taiping Island, which is one of Taiwan's possessions in the Spratlys. The island is fairly well populated and has its own hospital. While not coordinating its actions with the mainland, Taiwan is in agreement with the mainland in its refusal to accept the arbitration decision.

The political nature of the decision and the absence of China's indispensible consent to arbitration also undermined the credibility of the whole affair. Graham Allison, the Harvard professor who coined the term "Thucydides trap," said in an article in *The Diplomat* on July 11, that China can simply do as the United States and other powers have often done, and simply ignore the ruling—with impunity.

In one sense, the ball is now in the court of the new Philippine President, Rodrigo Duterte, who has clearly said that "war is not an option." Duterte has indicated all along that he wants to begin serious negotiations with China. When the ruling was issued, he asked former Philippine President Fidel Ramos to represent the Philippines in opening talks. Duterte is also eager to participate in the Belt and Road Initiative, which could provide the Philippines some of the much-needed infrastructure, particularly in the area of transportation, which it now lacks. But he will also come under a great deal of pressure from the United States to uphold the decision of the arbitration panel.

More important will be the direct reaction of the United States. If it continues to insist that China must forego its territorial claims, and continues to run its provocative reconnaissance operations under the guise of "freedom of navigation," this behavior will inevitably lead to a clash which can easily result in a full-scale military conflict.

And the ultimate target is China's ambitious attempt to bring the world back on the road to development through its Belt and Road Initiative. The success of the 21st Century Maritime Silk Road is dependent on a good working relationship with China's maritime neighbors, a relationship which can be seriously destabilized by this ruling.

Meanwhile, at the Asia-Europe Meeting (ASEM) in Ulaanbaatar, Mongolia, that ended on July 15, EU Chairman Donald Tusk began to discuss this arbitration ruling, greatly angering the Chinese delegation headed by Premier Li Keqiang, and leading to the sudden cancellation of the planned joint press conference.

President Rody Duterte Videos

Newly elected Philippine President Rodrigo Duterte, shown here on July 17, 2016, said that "war is not an option" in the fake South China Sea conflict.

As the Belt and Road Initiative offers the only real hope for Asia and Europe, and ultimately the United States, chastising China for not accepting this bogus ruling will have repercussions for all, confirming the warning State Councilor Yang gave to those trying to force China to give up its historical claims: "They are only lifting a stone to drop it on their own feet."

Lyndon LaRouche had seen these developments coming years ago. The instant he learned of Obama's brutal murder of Libyan leader Muammar al-Qaddafi on October 20, 2011, LaRouche exposed how and why it was that this atrocity indicated that Obama was rapidly lurching towards thermonuclear war against Russia and China.

Subsequent developments have amply confirmed that warning. Obama's "Pivot to Asia," a move towards war with China, was announced at just the same moment by Secretary of State Hillary Clinton. Now, at a moment when that war may be only weeks or days away, certain U.S. government figures have begun to waver. Obama can be contained and removed, and that war can be prevented, if we rally on an international scale for Lyndon and Helga Zepp-LaRouche's intiative, as presented in the July 15 webcast, "Bank Rescue Plan Is Last Chance." See page 5 of this issue.

SERGEY KARAGANOV

'We Don't Trust You in the Least … We Have To Find Ways To Revitalize Our Relations'

July 18—Sergey Karaganov is the head of the Russian Council on Foreign and Defense Policy, as well as the Dean of the Faculty of World Economy and International Affairs at Moscow's Higher School of Economics. He is also the past Deputy Director of the Institute of Europe at the Russian Academy of Sciences, and he served on the International Advisory Board of the Council on Foreign Relations from 1995 until 2005. Karaganov was a close associate, some might say protégé, of former Russian Prime Minister Yevgeny Primakov, and has been Presidential Adviser to both Boris Yeltsin and Vladimir Putin.

It would be a mistake to blindly attribute Karaganov's views to Russian President Putin, but he is a senior policy maker of the highest order in Moscow, and what he presents below is clearly indicative of the current outlook among many Russian leaders. Those in Europe and the United States who believe that Russia can be made to "bend" to the will of the trans-Atlantic alliance should pay close attention to what Mr. Karaganov says here.

What follows includes excerpts which are taken from an interview with Mr. Karaganov conducted by Christian Neef. The interview appeared in the German publication Der Spiegel, *on July 13, 2016.*

War Provocations in Europe

The interview begins with a series of questions pertaining to the ongoing escalation of NATO military deployments into Eastern Europe, and Karaganov is explicit that actions emanating from the West now pose an

CC/123presspress
Sergey Karaganov

existential threat to the Russian nation, that the posture and decisions being taken by European leaders are driving the situation toward war. He says:

> The situation has worsened considerably. We warned NATO against approaching the borders of Ukraine because that would create a situation that we cannot accept. Russia has stopped the Western advance in this direction and hopefully that means that the danger of a large war in Europe has been eliminated in the medium term. But the propaganda that is now circulating is reminiscent of the period preceding a new war…
> What is the West doing?

It is doing nothing but vilifying Russia; it believes that we are threatening to attack. The situation is comparable to the crisis at the end of the 1970s and beginning of the 1980s…

> Now, fears in countries like Poland, Lithuania and Latvia are to be allayed by NATO stationing weapons there. But that doesn't help them; we interpret that as a provocation. In a crisis, we will destroy exactly these weapons. Russia will never again fight on its own territory.

NATO Policy

The interview with Sergey Karaganov comes only weeks after "Operation Anakonda 16," a U.S.-Polish exercise that served as a conduit to bring in the forces of 19 NATO and 5 NATO partner countries, in Poland, which together with simultaneous NATO military maneuvers in the Baltic nations, represents the largest deployment of hostile military forces on Russia's western border since the Nazi invasion of 1941. These NATO "war games" have been denounced by Frank-Walter Steinmeier, the German Minister of Foreign Affairs, as well as other German and European leaders, as provocations which will solely have the effect of heightening war tensions.

On the subject of NATO, Karaganov declared:

Why is NATO stationing weapons and equipment there? Imagine what would happen to them in the case of a crisis. The help offered by NATO is not symbolic help for the Baltic states. It is a provocation. If NATO initiates an encroachment—against a nuclear power like ourselves—it will be punished...

NATO is no longer a legitimate body. Plus, NATO has become a qualitatively different alliance. When we began the dialogue with NATO, it was a defensive alliance of democratic powers. But then, the NATO-Russia Council served as cover for and the legalization of NATO expansion. When we really needed it—in 2008 and 2014—it wasn't there...

NATO is now 800 kilometers (497 miles) closer to the Russian border, weapons are completely different, strategic stability in Europe is shifting. Everything is much worse than it was 30 or 40 years ago.

The Eurasian Solution

Karaganov is explicit in the interview, that if Europe abandons its current hostile economic/military actions against Russia and seeks instead to find a path for cooperation and mutually beneficial relations, such an option exists. But no progress is possible unless there is a change of thinking in Europe.

The pathway out of the current confrontation was recently indicated at the July 25-26 Berlin Conference of the Schiller Institute, "A Common Future for Mankind and A Renaissance of Classical Culture." (See *EIR* issues July 1, July 8, and July 15). The proceedings of that historic event demonstrated that the idea of a community of nations acting on "the common goals of mankind" is indeed not a romantic chimera, but precisely what is already emerging in the form of the new Eurasian reality.

The dynamic expansion of economic investment through the Shanghai Cooperation Organization, the Chinese One Belt-One Road initiative, and the Eurasian Economic Union are all components of this new potential, and the presence and participation of Western European leaders in the recent St. Petersburg International Economic Forum is yet another sign that at least some of the European leadership recognizes this war avoidance path.

With regard to Russia's relations with Europe, Karaganov has this to say:

We currently find ourselves in a situation where we don't trust you [Europe] in the least, after all of the disappointments of recent years. And we are reacting accordingly. There is such a thing as tactical surprise. You should know that we are smarter, stronger, and more determined...

Many of my colleagues view our European partners with derision and I always warn them not to be cocky and arrogant. Some among the European elite have sought out confrontation with us. As a consequence, we won't help Europe, although we could do so when it comes to the refugee question. A joint closure of borders would be essential. In this regard, the Russians would be 10 times more effective than the Europeans. Instead, you have tried to make a deal with Turkey. That is a disgrace. In the face of our problems with Turkey, we have pursued a clear, hard political line—with success...

In Europe, you have a different political system, one that is unable to adapt to the challenges of the new world. The German Chancellor said that our president lives in a different world. I believe he lives in a very real world...

We believe that Russia is morally in the right. There won't be any fundamental concessions coming from our side. Psychologically, Russia has now become a Eurasian power—I was one of the intellectual fathers of the eastward pivot. But now I am of the opinion that we shouldn't turn away from Europe. We have to find ways to revitalize our relations.

The full interview with Sergey Karaganov can be found at http://www.spiegel.de/international/world/interview-with-putin-foreign-policy-advisor-sergey-karaganov-a-1102629.html

EDITORIAL

The One, Unique Link In the Chain

July 14—Forty-eight hours ago, we changed everything in our entire approach globally,—but many of you missed it. Think! Remind yourself that it's no use complaining about the immediate danger of a panic-collapse of the world economic system into deadly chaos. And mere warnings against a war of thermonuclear annihilation will not prevent it from happening anyway— any more than mere warnings ever prevented war in the past!

What Lyndon LaRouche has just done is to point to the one, unique link in the chain, which, if you grab ahold of *that*, and pull *that*, you may just then barely be able to pull Europe back from the precipice,— and, at the last possible moment, turn aside the mindless, automaton-like march of history over the abyss.

Put that off to think it over tomorrow, and you're done for! There will be no tomorrow,— for you or anyone.

All these considerations are laid out in Helga Zepp-LaRouche's statement of July 12, "Deutsche Bank Must be Rescued, for the Sake of World Peace." But many have not taken that statement to heart, and undertaken the immediate turnabout which is required.

Zepp-LaRouche's statement must be studied and re-studied in detail. But to recap some points for our purposes here: France, Italy, and the other European states are wholly bankrupt; Europe is heading for a blowout within days, which under present circumstances will lead to war. Germany's derivatives-laden Deutsche Bank may likely be the trigger-point for that Europe-wide blowout. But, paradoxically, it is precisely Germany which still has the potential economic productivity which could lead Europe back towards safety. And Deutsche Bank, if it were saved from collapse and immediately turned back towards the policies of Alfred Herrhausen, would be the lead agency in organizing such a German upsurge.

Lyndon LaRouche called for a government augmentation of Deutsche Bank's capital base, accompanied by an immediate reversal of its policies back to the Hamiltonian policies of Herrhausen. Simultaneously, a management committee must be appointed to sift through and reorganize the bank's assets.

During the past two days, many of our friends have exploded in rage at this life-saving proposal of Lyndon and Helga LaRouche, sputtering that the big banks are our enemies, and that we oppose bailouts. But as Diane Sare of the LaRouche PAC Policy Committee pointed out yesterday, it's really easy to recite a list of correct "positions." But what does that get you, other than a passport to Trotskyite Heaven? Far harder to understand and to seize the one last chance offered by history, as we must do now.

Those who murdered Herrhausen created an ongoing atrocity which has never ended to this day; those who did it have to be removed, or there is no solution. Sooner or later, something you hadn't done will come back to hit you.

www.ingramcontent.com/pod-product-compliance
Lightning Source LLC
Chambersburg PA
CBHW080325290526
45793CB00006B/1213